This book is dedicated to Bronte, Aaliyah and Safiyyah, and of course to the very remarkable Kashanito.

When Nature Calls,

Sea, Air and Land

Poems by
Ant Mac

This edition first published in paperback by
Michael Terence Publishing in 2023
www.mtp.agency

Copyright © 2023 Ant Mac

Ant Mac has asserted the right to be identified as
the author of this work in accordance with the
Copyright, Designs and Patents Act 1988

ISBN 9781800945760

Illustrations by
Ant Mac

Cover design
Copyright © 2023 Michael Terence Publishing

Michael Terence
Publishing

Sea

Air

Land

Sea

Water

The light spots drop before they pour,
A door was forced when hinges tore,
To blot a page and spread the run,
The stain that dried out in the sun,
The well filled well,
The surplus flowed,
The banks were burst to flood the hold,
Cold hands work fast to stem the leak,
With pressure's time and knees do creak,
The aches and pains when weather's damp,
The moisten sponge that sets the stamp,
For as it stands or bridged a plank,
The tread that dredges where less have sank,
Beyond the bells forebode the rank,
Above the frame that formed a prank,
A bucket kicked,
The list goes on,
Down through the pass,
Where odes were sung.

Fish

Hooked to avoid the line and batter,
What matters is the block that scales weigh,
The mouth that gasps seeks not to flatter,
For air it struggles in light of day.

Contort, confront, contract to wriggle,
In the middle of a sailor's sweet refrain,
Death sits upon an abated griddle,
Before the middle holds to contain.

Swim in the air in a desperate sequence,
Deceiving what the eye does see,
The surface below has lost all reason,
To suffocate while others breathe.

Writhe until the cradle holds,
The eyes are wide as the body sleeps,
Beneath the still the hand went cold,
Now on the surface what once was deep.

Decapitated and dissected,
Delivered unto many lands,
To agitate the source reflected,
Tend to a school to understand.

Sea Life

The ebb and flow,
and lapse of time,
a rhythm held like a summer's dance,
tied to a pull,
that swings and sways,
the lost buoy drifts on slowly.

Losing all energy,
and the will it never wrote,
or owned,
kelp it cries,
what is empty dies,
its efforts break a passage.

And salt the only sweet embrace,
a fleeting grace,
glanced towards the sun,
arms swim away and form to part,
the stroke upon each lesson.

A moon's harness and too release,
an empty vessel,
echoes and creaks,
secrets of the wind,
whisper ears to seek.

The mirrored ripple but a silhouette of hope,
chastised by the rise of fury,
they wave on and gulp mouthfuls of distaste,
weaned on brine and life's essence,
dipped and coated to break the surface,
with an oar,
or a quaint,
or a pen.

Calls of the deep,
locked in a struggle,
sharp for air again,
coming together to form bubbles,
rising like halos,
that float to desert you.

A wonder beheld,
dragged down for a privileged sight,
the body does fight as it tries to take flight,
far from a common resting ground,
the wings of an angel,
relinquish disparity.

Lifted up to the sun the light seems brighter than before,
less intrusive,
the buoyancy returns to the fore, for all to observe.

Carried away by the moment,
their eyes drop to sea as they scent,
losing touch with the horizon and all is absorbed as it
passes,
passes with no time to lament.

The River

Soft brooks bubble in gentle veins,
Press forth the spume a course it gains,
The tributes paid for meander's kiss,
To ward the ford of where inlets hid.

Wade on through towards a secret's bliss,
The rolling bank sank the hanging cliff,
Presents to drop with a fleeting glimpse,
The stone upturned reveals what others missed.

Chase, spurn and harry the water's fry,
To feed the current passing tide,
The pebble washed to soothe its coat,
What is released will rise and float.

A message wrote on bottles shipped,
Where rivers ran and chains were slipped,
Into the drink was over board,
A passage penned to pack what's stored.

What's to afford when guineas spent?
The price or prize down the river sent.

Memoirs of a Fish

Confused and caught,
I become removed and void,
I swim in the air in a death like sequence,
I writhe in suffocation with every twist and turn,
Swaying in the sun the heat does burn me,
Reflected against the backdrop,
I look down from the sky.

Crystalline sparkles blind me,
Nestled in a net I am cradled and carried away,
Carried from a home I loved and will never return,
Two hands bind around me and hold me still,
My value argued over and decided,
The voice of men agree my worth,
But what price is life and who should call it?
I express my pain in a secret language,
My voice travels back into the water,
To tell my brothers and sisters of their loss.

The Pirate

Drained and gaunt the complexion,
The composition for oppression perplexed,
To hunt and flaunt all insurrection,
Reflection haunts after its own neglect.

Brought to once deliver,
The liver an ounce or pound of flesh,
Caught to brace without trace or slither,
The giver brought more down to press.

Rest high in the bough that set creaking,
The shriek came from the teams cracking in the nest,
The glance beneath assailed sent fleeting,
A chance meeting was only seeking to escape
another's arrest.

Float to be buoyed by the current,
The drift in from past to present fast and sure,
Secure all strokes manned by the sullen,
Twitching to the last to at least reach the shore.

Air

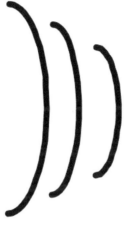

Air

What hangs and blows?
The wind will howl,
Deep breaths expand,
Deflate the ego,
Inflate to lift,
The buoyant mood,
A cloudy mist,
Kettles on thermals,
Kettles filled with steam,
Below help forms metal,
An atmosphere cut clean,
Expel from the system,
Exhaling through a tube,
The mask will aid oxygen.

Thunderstorm

Waves of rain,
Sweep in flurries,
The blurry curtains agitate the trees,
Their flaying branches attract attention,
Wind and water make nature freeze.

Electric spikes split the skies,
One thousand camera shutters close to capture frames,
The flashing strobes combined with rumbles and flutters,
Reaching from high,
To lord over the earth and stake a claim.

A primitive sound never altered or touched by time,
An alien language only the ancients can read,
We shelter and wait for the storm to climb,
To a point where distance tells us to breath.

Concentration

Inhale what is there,
Deeply shallow,
Gasping gulp,
To intake and expel,
Process to extract,
Swallow the rest,
Transfer and reuse,
For respiratory respite.

Despite the desperate chronic sighs,
Wearily weak,
From the weekly wear,
Sharp wisps,
Amount to composite percentages,
No concessions for shortness,
As the fight for breath becomes the battle,
The biggest lungs grab and need the most,
Though all are right and just.

Hierarchy has no order here,
Light-headedness takes on but the fortunate few,
Releasing what years of hurt are remembered,
Sharing with others,
Before expanding into one,
Falling into being many,
At least part of you escapes.

The Wasp

Contrasting colours merge in sight,
a flash with each flight,
the vibrancy might,
dampen the purr or hum,
that some succumb,
to listen dumb,
as it passes right,
before the eyes,
and those who wake,
light footsteps take,
to the water,
not breaking the surface,
or its purpose,
but for the slip of the tongue,
or a sip in the sun,
the head is hung,
down to drink or store,
to sink more,
and make secure,
for what's not absorbed,
is carried away,
with knowledge as key,
a symphony be,
like drone or worker,
free,

to seek out or roam,
or comb,
bound,
to hold its ground,
if confronted or contested,
the space infested,
unless given up and rejected,
before venom injected,
through a motion perfected,
leaving you reflective,
what's stung can be deceptive.

The Moth

What is mist in my demeanour,
Makes me fray when I am touched,
The thread is just a little leaner,
When the rug is pulled too much.

Adjust the light,
Reduce the glare,
The eyes will compensate the glow,
With just the right influx of air,
The breath will gently ease its flow.

Call from the candle,
The patterned handle,
Generates the heat of light,
And when it's bare weathered the vandal,
The iron brands you in the night.

Aware of the feast,
Release the craving,
The best will save it in a jar,
Wearers might warn us just by waving,
When our engraving made its mark.

A stark reality to territory,
We covert the dark to rest,
The part that sparks ignites our story,
And every fight is but a test.

Caressed the stretched out wing and body,
The rack and ruin of a maiden flight,
The pressed at best now torn and shoddy,
Unless the pest drifts to new heights.

Despite the knit of what was woven,
The proven cloth still dares to shred,
The holes return to join the stolen,
Fitting to nourish on what was said.

The Wood Pigeon

With or alone?
A path is chosen,
A judgment made to stay or go,
Safety hangs on all decision,
Without the vision who would know?

Within the open,
Leaved or sheltered,
Sometimes reside in the shade of trees,
Knowing where to search or forage,
Designed through signs that few can read.

At home in woodland,
Above the bracken,
The call is heard in light of day,
If words were spoken in human language,
I wonder what those words would say?

Opportunist or seasoned explorer?
Results out weigh the risks they take,
To disappear in early evening,
Tomorrow's fraught with plans to make.

The Fly

Waved off for being hungry,
A common viral need,
To layer in four corners,
To brush or paint with greed.

Waves of what will lure,
Drag most to draw their last,
A nuisance to the poor,
The bravest in the past.

Ways are set to poise,
Awaken on the stage,
When nature runs its course,
Some bottled up with rage.

Wade out upon the brine,
The hook was lined and sunk,
A raid upon the mind,
When fruit had made it drunk.

Search for justification,
Sensation in the verse,
To beaten elevation,
A strong sense made it worse.

Avoid the web or trap,
They are set to catch a stray,
Annoyed the knuckles rap,
Man aging to get away.

The Sparrow

The smallest squeeze without reduction,
The dart will take it swift and free,
On through the air the winged percussion,
With every flap the heart does beat.

The nimble swoop to search in numbers,
A warning scent along the breeze,
Their symbol proof to perch in slumber,
The morning sent to rustle leaves.

A chorus song to ease the breaking,
When gentle tunes summon the day,
With all among the spirit waking,
The gentile swoon leads it away.

Wait not for some with rapid flurry,
The peck was ordered to take its place,
And what succumbs to catch with worry,
Will flee the tree to find their space.

Bound to join and stick together,
Whether a simple fact or grace,
Braced to hit with changing weather,
As feathers dare to keep them safe.

The Seagull

Across the great expanse,
Elegance in motion,
To take a fleeting glance,
Feeling to flee the ocean.

Shadowing boats at sea,
Expertly waiting in the throng,
Looking back to see,
When those around you get it wrong.

Motoring on to land,
A parking lot a place to wait,
Escaping grains of sand,
To let descendants take the bait.

Pilfering on the periphery,
The pack will feed a hungry flock,
Mewing its own soliloquy,
Taking its fill and start to mock.

Pushed out to the regions,
Traversing in the air or ground,
Gathering in legions,
Feeding off what others found.

The Pigeon

The city bustle on your back,
When risky hustles spurn all tact,
A chancer's wrist to feed upon,
Or fancied risk to see undone.

Over the fence or on the wall?
The to and fro amidst the calls,
With strictest rules to roam the street,
The pavement stools to numb defeat.

Crowded house where others lay,
So more's the pity when they stay,
Under the bridge and on the ledge,
Jostled to place life on the edge.

Meagre portions challenged for,
A meal from scraps that urges more,
The rapid sounds as wings take flight,
The battlefield is lost from sight.

Urban dweller pushed and shunned,
Confined to lofts for warmth among,
Rafters wait with too much to bare,
After all, will all be treated fair?

The Magpie

Mechanical rattle bows to call,
And with its voice wakes one and all,
To set the stall to carry on,
With tales that stretch out when we're gone.

Beyond the realms where gold is claimed,
A feathered nest will take the blame,
When joy is found in another's sorrow,
The flush of silver awaits tomorrow.

Borrowed or stolen but rarely sold,
Just like that secret that's never told,
The mission clear to seek and search,
A watchful eye rests on its perch.

The Crow

Calling, falling cast a shadow,
Dark the pitted claw does dig,
Diving deep inside the shallow,
Rising above what others did.

Stark the teller of the story,
The bitter end will show no grace,
The battlefield still washed with glory,
Who won the fight to take their place?

What looms our sight in comprehension?
The tension holds us fast and tight,
Sit better pressed in cold contention,
And reappear in summer's flight.

Arrest the moment for its treasure,
The pressure closed to take a bite,
A universal mould to measure,
Weary from the dead of night.

Revered for ebony jet black feathers,
The weather bathed its inky gloss,
Rescue the clasp that holds the letter,
Or let it seek out those who lost.

Float higher still in sweet surrender,
A warning to those who hear, or think or feel,
The flesh is sharp the beak is tender,
Gently it's pressed impose it will.

Clay Pigeons

The grey reflected from the day,
A murky mist was on its way,
Towards the place where he will stay,
A bird in hand is what they say.

A chase to send it far away,
The grey reflected from the day,
The breeze might lean to gently sway,
Above the field in open play.

The light of sun does dance array,
The flight stayed right and never strayed,
The grey reflected from the day,
And then aligned the aim was made.

Caught in the air without delay,
The weakest hit the shell did spray,
The thunderous sound dispersing clay,
When grey reflected from the day.

Land

Earth

The sod that held its ground,
Battled frost and nightly invasion,
Bare and empty in the moon's gentle light,
Warm and content with the touch of the sun.

Dug and lifted by those wishing to exploit your giving nature,
You fold and facilitate all that they demand,
Offer shelter to the homeless and weary,
A resting place where some depart.

A bed you set a pretty sight,
Hands mould you into their interpretation of perfection,
When they are finished you look on and laugh,
Dance in the rain and take on a new form.

When life is over you crumble to dust,
Awaiting to be awoken,
So again you can be reborn.

The Soil

Laid, loosened, dug and settled,
The seed was nestled in the deep.

Pressed and watered from can or kettle,
We sow the ground for what we reap.

Drained and framed held in a border,
The walls absorbed within a trench.

The falling reign blamed for this order,
That footsteps filled when they were drenched.

The trudge a drudge to close the distance,
Persistence ploughed the loam a turn.

The root exposed yet more resistance,
Rotation helped them slash and burn.

Removed and staked the claim has risen,
The vessel placed to hear what's said.

For whom raked up all indecision,
The hallowed earth made him a bed.

Roots

What lies below stays hidden,
Its practise to absorb,
Pushed on to take what's given,
With every driven force.

Extract exact nutrition,
Proceed to fill the bed,
In fact the act's fruition,
Crept towards the water's edge.

Carried through veins and arteries,
Hold anchor to stand firm,
Food banked or gained its mastery,
Set over a can of worms.

To stretch and turn and tangle,
A twist to knot its last,
When girdling sits to strangle,
Insist to know the past.

The Leaf

New shoots sprout out,
uncurling as they spread,
fresh and green,
stretching up to greet the world,
growing bigger, stronger,
reaching, climbing,
open leaves like hands absorb what is given,
the sun's warm caress,
damp from the moist dew or rain,
sensitive to the touch.

Then limp with the loss of substance,
broken with inflexibility,
torn beyond repair,
aged and weathered from the toll that takes,
dead and devoid of life,
lost to the realms of yesterday,
forgotten by those who one day remarked,
on the potential,
and promise,
and marvelled on how I might grow.

Mutantur Folia

They tumble over one another,
Like acrobats that turn and spin,
Hide, before they are chased from cover,
Then carried off by force of wind.

Ejected from the sullen branches,
Released from where they once were held,
The fall will open up their chances,
Nature's urge again compelled.

Unapologetic by their arrival,
Turning up all different shades,
Played a part in our survival,
Now incomplete with edges frayed.

Broken down to leave just traces,
Kicked around and trampled on,
See the ground as season's faces,
Tell the tale of where they're from.

Elevation

Anticipating new light,
Like the plumule yearns for spring,
Rising up to view heights,
Find the urge to raise the chin.

A breakthrough from the loose earth,
With all resistance wearing thin,
Resettle on the surface,
No more waiting in the wings.

Daylight shines to ponder,
Awake the sleeping sense within,
The brows rise up in wonder,
With the eyes that take them in.

Across the seats of power,
Believe in you so now begin,
Beyond the darkest hour,
Like the plumule in the spring.

The Plant

If you could hear my voice,
Would you hear me beg for water?
One drop is all I need,
I would drink it all and waste nothing,
If on my knees I'd plead.

Would you hear me call for sunshine?
Some warmth and light would be nice,
A little time to drink in the day,
Until it reaches night.

Would you hear me ask for a soft bed,
In which I could rest and dream?
I wouldn't take from it the things I want,
But only the things I need.

Would you hear me cry for room to grow,
Enough to pretend that I'm free?
Not contained like a field or house plant,
Locked and held in misery.

The Flower

The flower sent to lure,
Dive to the nectar sink,
The liquid set to pour,
Had filled up to the brink.

The hour's scent was pure,
And paused the bee to drink,
Descend into the core,
To see the petals shrink.

What nature has in store,
Can cause the eye to blink,
The lesson here is more,
Imploring us to think.

The Tree

I started as a sapling,
planted in an open space,
I could see a big house with turrets that towered and
watched over me.
As a youngster, I saw men on horses gallop by,
small children would run around me,
the youngest of them would pull on my thin branches like
the hands of a friend.
I would bend and sigh,
and wished I could run.

At night I was lonely and sometimes cold.
After a few summers came and went,
brothers and sisters joined me.
I became the big brother and showed them how to grow.
The evenings became filled with talk as we passed
whispers about what we had seen in the day.

As my trunk grew thicker,
I was uprooted and moved,
closer to the big house.
My perimeter became encircled with high walls.
I didn't get to say goodbye.
And wished I could run.

After a while, a few of my siblings joined me and we spoke of the past.
I told them of what I had seen;
of ladies in dresses made of silk and velvet,
and of the jewels which they wore on their breasts and in their hair,
of the men who walked in shiny armour,
that told me of their approach way before they were in sight,
of how those children who once played about me,
and the one who would hold my hands,
now looked grown, elegant and bearded,
and how at night the rooms behind the stone walls on the floors above, flickered with candlelight and secrets.

One night there was panic in the eyes of the people around,
I felt the warmth of the fires that burnt out in the distance.
The sky glowed an orangey grey.
Screams were heard echoing through the night,
many people came and huddled around me,
faces I didn't recognise and voices I had never heard,
men clothed in metal ran in all directions,
and on the backs of horses raced from where I stood,
to the parts of the land that burned.
And wished I could run.

Leading them was that youngest child,
whose bearded face now came closer to me again,
he removed his glove and touched my bark before he left.
There was fear in his eyes.
When he returned tired and bloody it was almost light.
Fewer returned than the number who had left with him.
The fires died out on the hills,
yet the air was still thick and darkened with smoke,
and filled with the smell of burning.

Moons later,
the bearded man would come to sit beneath my canopy.
He would meet with others and talk with them about:
love, war and betrayal.
Over time I watched him as he began to age,
and his hair grew from brown to grey and from grey to
white.
His visits became less frequent,
until he was carried to me one last time.

He lay next to me as he took his last breath.
That was a sad day,
and one I will always remember.

My roots now stretched beyond the walls,
and I was reacquainted with the rest and more of my kin
I told them of my loss and they told me of theirs.
We comforted each other,
and I realised I could run.

Apples

A tree was grown and flattered,
The oath was from a seed,
Its bed on earth was scattered,
When a want became a need.

With innocence alluring,
Infectious to redeem,
An impudence grew during,
The life it gave to grieve.

Accepting admiration,
It stood where few will stand,
Add this to raw temptation,
Between woman and man.

When ripe it burst out secrets,
The flesh could not contain,
Its juice like blood secreted,
Then all around was stained.

The tempter was illusive,
And slipped off out of sight,
The penalty conducive,
What else was left to write?

A broken bough or promise,
Falls swiftly to the ground,
The gravity is honest,
And force to wear the crown.

The Flowering Oak

Caught, held fast and fixed in place,
The summer's whine of another lie,
When truth is plucked out from the air,
Up towards the sky the branch was bare.

What lullaby of velvet chord,
Could soothe the sayer? The crook was forged,
When mumbled words float out at night,
Help form a prayer for sin to fight.

Raised up to feel what hands will pull,
And break the bread till stomachs full,
Another rule that yoked a mule,
Or horse bolt shook a makeshift stool.

Haul take a weight,
A tightrope strained,
When nerves are frayed,
The fibres blamed.

Boots yanked and hung,
The dead of night,
The wisest fooled,
To see the light.

In cold of day,
They dare to lift,
What they have stolen,
Was not their gift.

The Yew Tree

You stand steady like a churchyard,
Long before the weight of stone,
Foundations nestled in your roots calmed,
And set to find a home.

Soothsayers conquer ages,
Some say the rings defeat,
The potent sap for sages,
Cradles ignorance to sleep.

Steer the wheel to Pilate,
Return to start again,
How bittersweet and silent,
And needle sharp the pen.

Macbeth tapped towards your secrets,
Secretions sat beneath the flesh,
The Bruce's boughs bent breaching,
When Bannockburn's bows bode best.

You stand steady while taproots search hard,
Long after the flight of cones,
Flesh nestled in the churchyard,
And now you stand alone.

The Olive Tree

Standing firm,
Gnarled and weathered,
Twisted arms contort to pray,
Roots in air,
Reach out to heaven,
The dusty green at dusk of day.

Silver felt enrobes the splendour,
Tender fruit unto the touch,
The flesh encased a stoic centre,
The bitter taste has grown too much.

Sheltered philosophers, prophets and poets,
Laid bare to witness what stows the seed,
The son of man shows how to enter,
And others pressed to watch it bleed.

With hands that shook the core's potential,
Some look to sit where others stand,
Picking up what's dropped is just sequential,
Another plant of what was planned.

The Apple Tree

In winter you lie dormant,
The frost lying on your back,
While you conserve your energy,
Waiting for change.

The spring,
Is a time of renewal and rebirth,
When your blossom is soft and delicate and fresh,
You call the honeybee to busy attention,
And she reciprocates.

In the summer you start to bring forth your fruit,
As your flower's petals fall away and disappear,
To reveal your bounty,
The sun brings a subtle sweetness to help mature
and intensify your allure,
Ripe and heavy on your bough,

Ready for the onset of autumn,
And for the gentle handshakes,
That pull and pluck,
Or until gravity persuades your laden branches
to part with their fruit,
To which you have given so much of you and your time.

Later you will sit there empty,
Saddened and in remission,
Like a father mourning his lost child,
Hoping they might return.

The seasons call your name and its cycle is relentless,
The days shorten with your contemplation,
Tired and weary,
You begin to sleep and dream,
Patiently waiting to awake.

The Money Tree

Coaxed by hands to conform aesthetics,
gentle persuasion helps form or weave a path,
soft and new leaves emerge to reach the light,
constrained and held within an observer's world of
control,
the canopy appears to hold freedom,
but the roots below stretch and fight for space,
growing tired and working ceaselessly,
the gentle creases in life do cry,
fingers that help,
open palms of dexterity,
ambidextrously wave,
tangle in a tiny web like that of a linyphiidae,
waiting for payment,
the shiny penny that turned bad.
Who said money doesn't grow on trees?

The Spider

Fight or faint in my presence?
The only essence is my lore,
A fowl stroke will only lessen,
A sound that deafens,
So here I roar.

Store not contempt for my demeanour,
The house looks cleaner when it's swept,
Throughout the night a silent weaver,
And pull the lever on what was left.

Stuck on lines just like a tightrope,
The cable stretched to bare all weight,
Struck on pine with any light hope,
The able wretch that bars the gate.

Deflate the buzz of an ego,
And clip the wings in many ways,
Elate the drudge of a beetle,
My kiss won't miss to steal the day.

Lair for the weary my disposition,
Sit in position to seal their fate,
Where others care and creep to listen,
Clockwork precision make muscles ache.

Running late upon a ladder,
The story sadder for minds to pay,
In awe for what was lost to fathom,
My form was given unto my prey.

The Ant

1

Every step light as a feather,
Across the grains or ridges deep,
Just as strong as she is clever,
As she appears to never sleep.

She walks for what we'd see as miles,
Sometimes alone to bridge a day,
Though she might stop once in a while,
She'll soon be back up on her way.

With confidence that's never dented,
Heightened senses help her stay in tune,
The surge of this can be relentless,
And faster still as she consumes.

She tries to live with many others,
Finding her place she'll play her part,
The home she built without her brothers,
And where she stops another starts.

2

Excavating a maze of tunnels,
Turning the corner to one who lays,
The bottle necked just like a funnel,
For that ensemble the tune is played.

Raised to the ground and full on sleeping,
Intruders creep to right and left,
The lost had found them softly weeping,
Commissions charged at a new depth.

To rubberstamp the channel's passage,
What leads them out to search and raid?
Against the crown the rivals banished,
When every challenge comes in its wake.

3

Escape the heart as wings are beating,
Above the soil he's on his way,
Although he may never be king,
He can be prince just for a day.

He travels on to find her chamber,
A guarded mouth carries him in,
If he is strong then throngs no danger,
The journey's cost was everything.

Free Lines

Upon the ledge next to a window,
Silent thoughts the watcher keeps,
Although you're close forever distant,
What fills your dreams when you're asleep?

Total world domination?
A simple stroke across the cheek?
Climbing trees or prowling rooftops?
Or basking in the summer's heat?

Freeing fish bones from a dustbin?
Chasing rivals in the street?
Scratch and hiss for your survival,
And always landing on your feet.

Tails or lives it's one too many,
Pouncing on what flies or tweets,
Hunting mice you're always ready,
Egyptians bound and held you deep.

Hitched on broomsticks they portrayed you,
Betrayed the imitation weak,
Familiarised by names they gave too,
Pause that thought before you leap.

The Fox

Chased, harassed and downtrodden,
Blamed with every curse,
Its home a concrete prison,
Since justice was dispersed.

Shying from the limelight,
The moonlight flashes on its toes,
With energy enough to climb heights,
When life's entangled with its foes.

The hound or dreaded beagle,
Enter the chase so bred,
From working hand to regal,
No safe place for a bed.

Some said it was genetic,
A custom to the law,
The weary dog still hunted,
Until the spirit raw.

Implore the rhyme to reason,
The season's change is fast,
Imagine if odds were even,
And all mistreatment in the past.

The Polar Bear

They flock in droves to stand and stare,
The bitter truth abounds,
The locked in cove that brands to tear,
What sits aloof falls down.

Fear to release and lose its glow,
Capture a sorrowful projection,
They preach protection but what do they know,
A passed down imperfection.

Reflection on the flakes of snow,
Or better deep set ivory,
The strength upon the steel does show,
It wrestled inner rivalry.

Confined to the coat of the skin,
Its presence held fixed rotation,
Constructed there a folly within,
And the farce its consolation.

The pole was stolen,
Lost and torn,
The spirit held and dented,
Pools of the day,
Where dreams were born,
When only souls relented.

Its elevation comes from the pen,
The eyes cast down the flaw,
The desolation leans towards its kin,
The wise pass to no more.

The Snail

Slow moving to a greater distance,
Persistence is my inner strength,
To drift upon the road's resistance,
Outward consistence raised my head.

The foot will dare to run the gauntlet,
Pressed down to where they watch me tread,
A passage smooth and trail flaunted,
The passing soothes a jagged ledge.

Leaves languish damp in mottled shelter,
I heave and breathe out where I stop,
The leaf upturned to what is selfish,
Desperate the urge to run a mock.

Flock around the feast,
Just like a seagull,
Light reflects on every crease,
The forage finds its own elation,
A fascination to reach its feat.

Beat with the blood in circulation,
When navigation is its own discourse,
Inching the miles to a validation,
Emancipated until I'm caught.

The Beetle

The shell encased and protected,
A reflected inner space,
Shelters from what is defective,
And the pressure that pushes its pace.

Self navigate towards a compass,
That passes a channel to break,
To say it's by chance is presumptuous,
The soil that shook in its wake.

Take up the shovel and dig,
The truth is revealed hidden there,
Prize up, search under the lid,
To find where it buried its share.

Click or tap in June,
Reassemble the tune to march,
Too soon a threat will loom,
And presume to prune the last.

The dye was cast like iron,
Fixated on the role of tormentor,
And I for want of trying,
Watch over the great coleoptera.

The Pigeon Fancier

The loss of light paid close attention,
And not to mention the motion slow,
The flow was low for comprehension,
As all retention had made it so.

His hands pressed down to prune their
structure,
Towards the lustre was pushed to aim,
The time was held for rules to muster,
With blustered winds that lost his name.

The form was bent from repetition,
This fixed position of twisted frame,
Out of the hat a tricked magician,
Let indecision take all the blame.

And such a gift to home a pigeon,
But this a prison to fly from touch,
Upon the prize his eye lid risen,
Towards a vision that lost so much.

A fledgling trained and flew the coup,
And then regrouped to take in stock,
Sift out the grain for those who stoop,
Signal the troops who stayed aloft.

On the front foot far behind them,
Aligned, his memory served him well,
He bore the brunt while some reminded,
The Dickin medal least made him swell.

Returned to rent and now retired,
Spirit desired and promised more,
The breathing slow the voice now silent,
An inner tyrant had swept the floor.

About the Author

Ant Mac is a poet and writer, who writes for both adults and children. He has been writing stories and poetry for more years than he cares to remember. His work has been published in numerous magazines, journals and anthologies.

When not writing, Ant Mac likes to immerse himself into books whether this is reading them in his spare time or marking them when he is at work as a teacher.

Ant Mac has also written two children's books:

The Tale of Little Beak

Toby and Ben.

Available worldwide from Amazon
and all good bookstores

———————

Michael Terence
Publishing

www.mtp.agency

www.facebook.com/mtp.agency

@mtp_agency